Maxims
From Francois Fenelon
Archbishop of Cambray
By
Francois Fenelon

Translated by
Thomas C Upham

St Athanasius Press
All Rights Reserved 2018

ISBN-13: 978-1719076975

ISBN-10: 1719076979

St Athanasius Press
melwaller@gmail.com

Specializing in
Reprinting Catholic Classics

All Rights Reserved 2018

Maxims of the Saints From Francois Fenelon In 45 Articles

ARTICLE FIRST

Of the love of God, there are various kinds. At least, there are various feelings which go under that name.

First, There is what may be called mercenary or selfish love; that is, that love of God which originates in a sole regard to our own happiness. Those who love God with no other love than this, love Him just as the miser his money, and the voluptuous man his pleasures; attaching no value to God, except as a means to an end; and that end is the gratification of themselves. Such, love, if it can be called by that name, is unworthy of God. He does not ask it; He will not receive it. In the language of Francis de Sales, "it is sacrilegious and impious."

Second, Another kind of love does not exclude a regard to our own happiness as a motive of love, but requires this motive to be subordinate to a much higher one, namely, that of a regard to God's glory. It is a mixed state, in which we regard ourselves and God at the same time. This love is not necessarily selfish and wrong. On the contrary, when the two objects of it, God and ourselves, are relatively in the right position, that is to say, when we love God as He ought to be loved, and love ourselves no more than we ought to be loved, it is a love which, in being properly subordinated, is unselfish and is right.

ARTICLE SECOND

I. Of the subjects of this mixed love all are not equally advanced.

II. Mixed love becomes pure love, when the love of self is relatively, though not absolutely, lost in a regard to the will of God. This is always the case, when the two objects are loved in their due proportion. So that pure love is mixed love when it is combined rightly.

III. Pure love is not inconsistent with mixed love, but is mixed love carried to its true result. When this result is attained, the motive of God's glory so expands itself, and so fills the mind, that the other motive, that of our own happiness, becomes so small, and so recedes from our inward notice, as to be practically annihilated. It is then that God becomes what He ever ought to be the center of the soul, to which all its affections tend; the great moral sun of the soul, from which all its light and all its warmth proceed. It is then that a man thinks no more of himself. He has become the man of a "single eye." His own happiness, and all that regards himself, is entirely lost sight of in his simple and fixed look to God's will and God's glory.

IV. We lay ourselves at His feet. Self is known no more; not because it is wrong to regard and to desire our own good, but because the object of desire is withdrawn from our notice. When the sun shines, the stars disappear. When God is in the soul who can think of himself? So that we love God, and God alone; and all other things in and for God.

ARTICLE THIRD

In the early periods of religious experience, motives, which have a regard to our personal happiness, are more prominent and effective than at later periods; nor are they to be condemned. It is proper, in addressing even religious men, to appeal to the fear of death, to the impending judgments of God, to the terrors of hell and the joys of heaven. Such appeals are recognized in the Holy Scriptures, and are in accordance with the views and feelings of good men in all ages of the world. The motives involved in them are powerful aids to beginners in religion; assisting, as they do, very much in repressing the passions, and in strengthening the practical virtues.

We should not think lightly, therefore, of the grace of God, as manifested in that inferior form of religion which stops short of the more glorious and perfected form of pure love. We are to follow God's grace, and not to go before it. To the higher state of pure love we are to advance step by step; watching carefully God's inward and outward providence; and receiving increased grace by improving the grace we have, till the dawning light becomes the perfect day.

ARTICLE FOURTH

He who is in the state of pure or perfect love, has all the moral and Christian virtues in himself. If temperance, forbearance, chastity, truth, kindness, forgiveness, justice, may be regarded as virtues, there can be no doubt that they are all included in holy love. That is to say, the principle of love will not fail to develop itself in each of these forms. St. Augustine remarks, that love is the foundation, source, or principle of all the virtues. This view is sustained also by St. Francis de Sales and by Thomas Aquinas.

The state of pure love does not exclude the mental state which is called Christian hope. Hope in the Christian, when we analyze it into its elements, may be described as the desire of being united with God in heaven, accompanied with the expectation or belief of being so.

ARTICLE FIFTH

Souls that, by being perfected in love, are truly the subjects of sanctification, do not cease, nevertheless, to grow in grace. It may not be easy to specify and describe the degrees of sanctification; but there seem to be at least two modifications of experience after persons have reached this state.

1. The first may be described as the state of holy resignation. Such a soul thinks more frequently than it will, at a subsequent period, of its own happiness.

2. The second state is that of holy indifference. Such a soul absolutely ceases either to desire or to will, except in cooperation with the Divine leading. Its desires for itself, as it has greater light, are more completely and permanently merged in the one higher and more absorbing desire of God's glory, and the fulfillment of His will. In this state of experience, ceasing to do what we shall be likely to do, and what we may very properly do in a lower state, we no longer desire our own salvation merely as an eternal deliverance, or merely as involving the greatest amount of personal happiness; but we desire it chiefly as the fulfillment of God's pleasure, and as resulting in His glory, and because lie Himself desires and wills that we should thus desire and will.

3. Holy indifference is not inactivity. It is the fur-

thest possible from it. It is indifference to anything and everything out of God's will; but it is the highest life and activity to anything and everything in that will.

ARTICLE SIXTH

One of the clearest and best established maxims of holiness is, that the holy soul, when arrived at the second state mentioned, ceases to have desires for anything out of the will of God. The holy soul, when it is really in the state called the state of non-desire, may, nevertheless, desire everything in relation to the correction of its imperfections and weaknesses, its perseverance in its religious state, and its ultimate salvation, which it has reason to know from the Scriptures, or in any other way, that God desires. It may also desire all temporal good, houses and lands, food and clothing, friends and books, and exemption from physical suffering, and anything else, so far and only so far, as it has reason to think that such desire is coincident with the Divine desire. The holy soul not only desires particular things, sanctioned by the known will of God; but also the fulfillment of His will in all respects, unknown as well as known. Being in faith, it commits itself to God in darkness as well as in light. Its non-desire is simply its not desiring anything out of God

ARTICLE SEVENTH

In the history of inward experience, we not infrequently find accounts of individuals whose inward life may properly be characterized as extraordinary. They represent themselves as having extraordinary communications; dreams, visions, revelations. Without stopping to inquire whether these inward results arise from an excited and disordered state of the physical system or from God, the important remark to be made here is, that these things, to whatever extent they may exist, do not constitute holiness.

The principle, which is the life of common Christians in their common mixed state, is the principle which originates and sustains the life of those who are truly "the pure in heart," namely, the principle of faith working by love,--existing, however, in the case of those last mentioned, in a greatly increased degree. This is obviously the doctrine of John of the Cross, who teaches us, that we must walk in the night of faith; that is to say, with night around us, which exists in consequence of our entire ignorance of what is before us, and with faith alone, faith in God, in His Word, and in his Providences, for the soul's guide.

Again, the persons who have, or are supposed to have, the visions and other remarkable states to which we have referred are sometimes disposed to make their own experience, imperfect as it obviously is, the guide of their life, considered as separate from and as above the written law. Great care should be taken against such an error as this. God's word is our true rule.

Nevertheless, there is no interpreter of the Divine Word like that of a holy heart; or, what is the same thing, of the Holy Ghost dwelling in the heart. If we give ourselves wholly to God, the Comforter will take up His abode with us, and guide us into all that truth which will be necessary for us. Truly holy souls, therefore, continually looking to God for a proper understanding of His Word, may confidently trust that He will guide them aright. A holy soul, in the exercise of its legitimate powers of interpretation, may deduce important views from the Word of God which would not otherwise be known; but it cannot add anything to it.

Again, God is the regulator of the affections, as well as of the outward actions. Sometimes the state which He inspires within us is that of holy love;- sometimes He inspires affections which have love and faith for their basis, but have a specific character, and then appear under other names, such as humility, forgiveness, gratitude. But in all cases there is nothing holy, except what is based upon the antecedent or "prevenient" grace of God. In all the universe, there is hut one legitimate Originator. Man's business is that of concurrence. And this view is applicable to all the stages of Christian experience, from the lowest to the highest.

ARTICLE EIGHTH

Writers often speak of abandonment. The term has a meaning somewhat specific. The soul in this state does not renounce everything, and thus become brutish in its indifference; but renounces everything except God's will.

Souls in the state of abandonment, not only forsake outward things, but, what is still more important, forsake themselves.

Abandonment, or self-renunciation, is not the renunciation of faith or of love or of anything else, except selfishness.

The state of abandonment, or entire self-renunciation, is generally attended, and perhaps we may say, carried out and perfected, by temptations more or less severe. We cannot well know, whether we have renounced ourselves, except by being tried on those very points to which our self-renunciation, either real or supposed, relates. One of the severest inward trials is that by which we are taken off from all inward sensible supports, and are made to live and walk by faith alone. Pious and holy men who have been the subjects of inward crucifixion, often refer to the trials which have been experienced by them. They sometimes speak of them as a sort of inward and terrible purgatory. "Only mad and wicked men," says Cardinal Bona, "will deny the existence of these remarkable experiences, attested as they are by men of the most venerable virtue, who speak only of what they have known in themselves."

Trials are not always of the same duration. The more cheerfully and faithfully we give ourselves to God, to be smitten in any and all of our idols, whenever and wherever He chooses, the shorter will be the work. God makes us to suffer no longer than He sees to be necessary for us.

We should not be premature in concluding that inward crucifixion is complete, and our abandonment to God is without any reservation whatever. The act of consecration, which is a sort of incipient step, may be sincere; but the reality of the consecration can be known only when God has applied the appropriate tests. The trial will show whether we are wholly the Lord's. Those who prematurely draw the conclusion that they are so, expose themselves to great illusion and injury.

ARTICLE NINTH

The state of abandonment, or of entire self-renunciation, does not take from the soul that moral power which is essential to its moral agency; nor that antecedent or prevenient grace, without which even abandonment itself would be a state of moral death; nor the principle of faith, which prevenient grace originated, and through which it now operates; nor the desire and hope of final salvation, although it takes away all uneasiness and unbelief connected with such a desire; nor the fountains of love which spring up deeply and freshly within it; nor the hatred of sin; nor the testimony of a good conscience.

But it takes away that uneasy hankering of the soul after pleasure either inward or outward, and the selfish vivacity and eagerness of nature, which is too impatient to wait calmly and submissively for God's time of action. By fixing the mind wholly upon God, it takes away the disposition of the soul to occupy itself with reflex acts; that is, with the undue examination and analysis of its own feelings. It does not take away the pain and sorrow naturally incident to our physical state and natural sensibilities; but it takes away all uneasiness, all murmuring; leaving the soul in its inner nature, and in every part of its nature where the power of faith reaches, calm and peaceable as the God that dwells there.

ARTICLE TENTH

God has promised life and happiness to His people. What He has promised can never fail to take place. Nevertheless, it is the disposition of those who love God with a perfect heart, to leave themselves entirely in His hands, irrespective, in some degree, of the promise. By the aid of the promise, without which they must have remained in their original weakness, they rise, as it were, above the promise; and rest in that essential and eternal will, in which the promise originated.

So much is this the case, that some individuals, across whose path God had spread the darkness of His providences, and who seemed to themselves for a time to be thrown out of His favor and to be hopelessly lost, have acquiesced with submission in the terrible destiny which was thus presented before them. Such was the state of mind of Francis de Sales, as he prostrated himself in the church of St. Stephen des Grez. The language of such persons, uttered without complaint, is, "My God, my God, why hast thou forsaken me?" They claim God as their God, and will not abandon their love to Him, although they believe, at the time, that they are forsaken of Him. They choose to leave themselves, under all possible circumstances, entirely in the hands of God: their language is, even if it should be His pleasure to separate them for ever from the enjoyments of His presence, Not my will, but thine be done."

It is perhaps difficult to perceive, how minds whose life, as it were, is the principle of faith, can be in this situation. Take the case of the Saviour. It is certainly difficult to conceive how the Saviour, whose faith never failed, could yet believe Himself forsaken; and yet it was so.

We know that it is impossible for God to forsake those who put their trust in Him. He can just as soon forsake His own word; and, what is more, He can just as soon forsake His own nature. Holy souls, nevertheless, may sometimes, in a way and under circumstances which we may not fully understand, believe themselves to be forsaken, beyond all possibility of hope; and yet such is their faith in God arid their love to Him, that the will of God, even under such circumstances, is dearer to them than anything and everything else.

ARTICLE ELEVENTH

One great point of difference between the First Covenant, or the covenant of works, which said to men, "Do this and live," and the Second Covenant, or the covenant of grace, which says, Believe and live," is this: The first covenant did not lead men to anything that was perfect. It showed men what was right and good; but it failed in giving them the power to fulfill what the covenant required. Men not only understood what was right and good, but they knew what was evil; but, in their love and practice of depravity, they had no longer power of themselves to flee from it.

The new or Christian covenant of grace, not only prescribes and commands, but gives also the power to fulfill.

In the practical dispensations of divine grace, there are number of principles which it may be important to remember.

1. God being LOVE, it is a part of His nature to desire to communicate Himself to all moral beings, and to make Himself one with them in a perfect harmony of relations and feelings. The position of God is that of giver; the position of man is that of recipient. harmonized with man by the blood and power of the Cross, he has once more become the infinite

fullness, the original and overflowing fountain, giving and ever ready to give.

2. Such are the relations between God and man, involved in the fact of man's moral agency, that man's business is to receive.

3. Souls true to the grace given them, will never suffer any diminution of it. On the contrary, the great and unchangeable condition of continuance and of growth in grace is cooperation with what we now have. This is the law of growth, not only deducible from the Divine nature, but expressly revealed and declared in the Scriptures: "For whosoever hath, to him shall be given, and he shall have more abundance; but whosoever hath not, from him shall be taken away even that he hath."-Matt. xiii. 12.

A faithful cooperation with grace, is the most effectual preparation for attracting and receiving and increasing grace. This is the great secret of advancement to those high degrees which are permitted; namely, a strict, unwavering, faithful cooperation, moment by moment.

4. It is important correctly to understand the doctrine of cooperation. A disposition to cooperate, is not more opposed to the sinful indolence which falls behind, than to the hasty and unrighteous zeal which runs before. It is in the excess of zeal, which has a

good appearance, but in reality has unbelief and self at the bottom, that we run before God.

5. Cooperation, by being calm and peaceable, does not cease to be efficacious. Souls in this purified but tranquil state are souls of power; watchful and triumphant against self; resisting temptation; fighting even to blood against sin. But it is, nevertheless, a combat free from the turbulence and inconsistencies of human passion; because they contend in the presence of God, who is their strength, in the spirit of the highest faith and love, and under the guidance of the Holy Ghost, who is always tranquil in His operations.

ARTICLE TWELFTH

Those in the highest state of religions experience desire nothing, except that God may be glorified in them by the accomplishment of His holy will. Nor is it inconsistent with this, that holy souls possess that natural love which exists in the form of love for themselves. Their natural love, however, which, within its proper degree, is innocent love, is so absorbed in the love of God, that it ceases, for the most part, to be a distinct object of consciousness; and practically and truly they may be said to love themselves IN and FOR God. Adam, in his state of innocence, loved himself, considered as the reflex image of God and for God's sake. So that we may either say, that he loved God in himself, or that he loved himself IN and FOR God. And it is because holy souls, extending their affections beyond their own limit, love their neighbor on the same principle of loving, namely, IN and FOR God, that they may be said to love their neighbors as themselves.

It does not follow, because the love of ourselves is lost in the love of God, that we are to take no care, and to exercise no watch over ourselves. No man will be so seriously and constantly watchful over himself as he who loves himself IN and FOR God alone. Having the image of God in himself, he has a motive strong, we might perhaps say, as that which controls the actions of angels, to guard and protect it.

It may be thought, perhaps, that this is inconsistent with the principle in the doctrines of holy living, which requires in the highest stages of inward experience, to avoid those reflex acts which consist in self-inspection, because such acts have a tendency to turn the mind off from God. The apparent difficulty is reconciled in this way. The holy soul is a soul with God; moving as God moves; doing as God does; looking as God looks. If, therefore, God is looking within us, as we may generally learn from the intimations of His providences, then it is a sign that we are to look within ourselves. Our little eye, our small and almost imperceptible ray, must look in, in the midst of the light of His great and burning eye. It is thus that we may inspect ourselves without a separation from God.

On the same principle, we may be watchful and careful over our neighbors; watching them, not in our own time, but in God's time; not in the censoriousness of nature, but in the kindness and forbearance of grace; not as separate from God, but in concurrence with Him.

ARTICLE THIRTEENTH

The soul, in the state of pure love, acts in simplicity. Its inward rule of action is found in the decisions of a sanctified conscience. These decisions, based upon judgments that are free from self-interest, may not always be absolutely right, because our views and judgments, being limited, can extend only to things in part; but they may be said to be relatively right: they conform to things so far as we are permitted to see them and understand them, and convey to the soul a moral assurance, that, when we act in accordance with them, we are doing as God would have us do. Such a conscience is enlightened by the Spirit of God; and when we act thus, under its Divine guidance, looking at what now is and not at what may be, looking at the right of things and not at their relations to our personal and selfish interests, we are said to act in simplicity. This is the true mode of action.

Thus, in this singleness of spirit, we do things, as some experimental writers express it, without knowing what we do. We are so absorbed in the thing to be done, and in the importance of doing it rightly, that we forget ourselves. Perfect love has nothing to spare from its object for itself, and he who prays perfectly is never thinking how well he prays.

ARTICLE FOURTEENTH

Holy souls are without impatience, but not without trouble; are above murmuring, but not above affliction. The souls of those who are thus wholly in Christ may be regarded in two points of view, or rather in two parts; namely, the natural appetites, propensities, and affections, on the one hand, which may be called the inferior part; and the judgment, the moral sense, and the will, on the other, which may be described as the superior part. As things are, in the present life, those who are wholly devoted to God may suffer in the inferior part, and may be at rest in the superior. Their wills may be in harmony with the Divine will; they may be approved in their judgments and conscience, and at the same time may suffer greatly in their physical relations, and in their natural sensibilities. In this manner, Christ upon the cross, while His will remained firm in its union with the will of His heavenly Father, suffered much through His physical system; He felt the painful longings of thirst, the pressure of the thorns, and the agony of the spear. He was deeply afflicted also for the friends He left behind Him, and for a dying world. But in His inner and higher nature, where He felt Himself sustained by the secret voice uttered in His sanctified conscience and in His unchangeable faith, He was peaceful and happy.

ARTICLE FIFTEENTH

A suitable repression of the natural appetites is profitable and necessary. We are told that the body should be brought into subjection. Those physical mortifications, therefore, which are instituted to this end, denominated austerities, are not to be disapproved. When practiced within proper limits, they tend to correct evil habits, to preserve us against temptation, and to give self-control.

The practice of austerities, with the views and on the principles indicated, should be accompanied with the spirit of recollection, of love, and prayer. Christ himself, whose retirement to solitary places, whose prayers and fastings are not to be forgotten, has given us the pattern which it is proper for us to follow. We must sometimes use force against our stubborn nature. "Since the days of John, the kingdom of heaven suffers violence; and the violent take it by force."

ARTICLE SIXTEENTH

The simple desire of our own happiness, kept in due subordination, is innocent. This desire is natural to us; and is properly denominated the principle of SELF-LOVE. When the principle of self-love passes its appropriate limit, it becomes selfishness. Self-love is innocent; selfishness is wrong. Selfishness was the sin of the first angel, "who rested in himself," as St. Augustine expresses it, instead of referring himself to God.

In many Christians a prominent principle of action is the desire of happiness. They love God and they love heaven; they love holiness, and they love the pleasures of holiness; they love to do good, and they love the rewards of doing good. This is well; but there is something better. Such Christians are inferior to those who forget the nothingness of the creature in the infinitude of the Creator, and love God for His own glory alone.

ARTICLE SEVENTEENTH

No period of the Christian life is exempt from temptation. The temptations incident to the earlier stages are different from those incident to a later period, and are to be resisted in a different manner.

Sometimes the temptations incident to the transition-state from mixed love to pure love are somewhat peculiar, being adapted to test whether we love God for Himself alone.

In the lower or mixed state the methods of resisting temptations are various. Sometimes the subject of these trials boldly faces them, and endeavors to overcome them by a direct resistance. Sometimes he turns and flees. But in the state of pure love, when the soul has become strong in the Divine contemplation, it is the common rule laid down by religious writers, that the soul should keep itself fixed upon God in the exercise of its holy love as at other times, as the most effectual way of resisting the temptation, which would naturally expand its efforts in vain upon a soul in that state.

ARTICLE EIGHTEENTH

The will of God is the ultimate and only rule of action. God manifests His will in various ways. The will of God may in some cases be ascertained by the operations of the human mind, especially when under a religious or gracious guidance. But He reveals His will chiefly in His written word. And nothing can be declared to be the will of God, which is at variance with His written or revealed will, which may also be called His positive will.

If we sin, it is that that God permits it; but it is also true, that He disapproves and condemns it as contrary to His immutable holiness.

It is the business of the sinner to repent. The state of penitence has temptations peculiar to itself. He is sometimes tempted to murmuring and rebellious feelings, as if he had been unjustly left of God. When penitence is true, and in the highest state, it is free from the variations of human passion.

ARTICLE NINETEENTH

Among other distinctions of prayer, we may make that of vocal and silent, the prayer of the lips and the prayer of the affections. Vocal prayer, without the heart attending it, is superstitious and wholly unprofitable. To pray without recollection in God and without love, is to pray as the heathen did, who thought to be heard for the multitude of their words.

Nevertheless, vocal prayer, when attended by right affections, ought to be both recognized and encouraged, as being calculated to strengthen the thoughts and feelings it expresses, and to awaken new ones, and also for the reason that it was taught by the Son of God to His Apostles, and that it has been practiced by the whole Church in all ages. To make light of this sacrifice of praise, this fruit of the lips, would be an impiety.

Silent prayer, in its common form, is also profitable. Each has its peculiar advantages, as each has its place.

There is also a modification of prayer, which may be termed the prayer of silence. This is a prayer too deep for words. The common form of silent prayer is voluntary. In the prayer of contemplative silence, the lips seem to be closed almost against the will.

ARTICLE TWENTIETH

The principles of holy living extend to everything. For instance, in the matter of reading, he who has given himself wholly to God, can read only what God permits him to read. He cannot read books, however characterized by wit or power, merely to indulge an idle curiosity, or to please himself alone.

In reading this may be a suitable direction, namely, to read but little at a time, and to interrupt the reading by intervals of religious recollection, in order that we may let the Holy Spirit more deeply imprint in us Christian truths.

God, in the person of the Holy Ghost, becomes to the fully renovated mind the great inward Teacher. This is a great truth. At the same time we are not to suppose that the presence of the inward teacher exempts us from the necessity of the outward lesson. The Holy Ghost, operating through the medium of a purified judgment, teaches us by the means of books, especially by the word of God, which is never to be laid aside.

ARTICLE TWENTY-FIRST

One characteristic of the lower states of religious experience is, that they are sustained, in a considerable degree, by meditative and reflective acts. As faith is comparatively weak and temptations are strong, it becomes necessary to gain strength by such meditative and reflective acts, by the consideration of various truths applicable to their situation, and of the motives drawn from such truths. Accordingly, souls array before them all the various motives drawn from the consideration of misery on the one hand, and of happiness on the other; all the motives of fear and hope.

It is different with those who have given themselves wholly to God in the exercise of pure or perfect love. The soul does not find it necessary to delay and to meditate, in order to discover motives of action. It finds its motive of action a motive simple, uniform, peaceable, and still powerful beyond any other power, in its own principle of life.

Meditation, inquiry, and reasoning, are exceedingly necessary to the great body of Christians; and absolutely indispensable to those in the beginnings of the Christian life. To take away these helps would be to take away the child from the breast before it can digest solid food. Still they are only the props, and not the life itself.

ARTICLE TWENTY-SECOND

The holy soul delights in acts of contemplation; to think of God and of God only. But the contemplative state, without any interruption, is hardly consistent with the condition of the present life. It may be permitted to exist, however, and ought not to be resisted, when the attraction towards God is so strong, that we find ourselves incapable of profitably employing our minds in meditative and discursive acts.

ARTICLE TWENTY-THIRD

Of the two states, the meditative and discursive on the one hand, which reflects, compares, and reasons, and supports itself by aids and methods of that nature, and the contemplative on the other, which rests in God without such aids, the contemplative is the higher. God will teach the times of both. Neither state is, or ought to be, entirely exclusive of the other.

ARTICLE TWENTY-FOURTH

In some cases God gives such eminent grace, that the contemplative prayer, which is essentially the same with the prayer of silence, becomes the habitual state. We do not mean, that the mind is always in this state; but that, whenever the season of recollection and prayer returns, it habitually assumes the contemplative state, in distinction from the meditative and discursive.

It does not follow that this state, eminent as it is, is invariable. Souls may fall from this state by some act of infidelity in themselves; or God may place them temporarily in a different state.

ARTICLE TWENTY-FIFTH

"Whether, therefore," says the Apostle, "you eat or drink, or whatsoever you do, do all things to the glory of God," 1 Cor. X. 31. And in another passage he says, "Let all things be done with charity," 1 Cor. XVI. 14. And again, "By love serve one another," Gal. V.13: passages which, with many others, imply two things; first, that everything which is done by the Christian ought to be done from a holy principle; and, second, that this principle is love.

ARTICLE TWENTY SIXTH

Our acceptance with God, when our hearts are wholly given to Him, does not depend upon our being in a particular state, but simply upon our being in that state in which God in His providence requires us to be. The doctrine of holiness, therefore, while it recognizes and requires, on its appropriate occasions, the prayer of contemplation or of contemplative silence, is not only not inconsistent with other forms of prayer, but is not at all inconsistent with the practice of the ordinary acts, duties, and virtues of life. It would be a great mistake to suppose, that a man who bears the Saviour's image, is any the less on that account a good neighbor or a good citizen; that he can think less or work less when he is called to it; or that he is not characterized by the various virtues, appropriate to our present situation, of temperance, truth, forbearance, forgiveness, kindness, chastity, justice. There is a law, involved in the very nature of holiness, which requires it to adapt itself to every variety of situation.

ARTICLE TWENTY-SEVENTH

It is in accordance with the views of Dionysius the Areopagite, to say, that the holy soul in its contemplative state, is occupied with the pure or spiritual Divinity. That is to say, it is occupied with God, in distinction from any mere image of God, such as could be addressed to the touch, the sight, or any of the senses.

And this is not all. It does not satisfy the desires of the soul in its contemplative state, to occupy itself merely with the attributes of God; with His power, wisdom, goodness, and the like; but it rather seeks and unites itself with the God of the attributes. The attributes of God are not God himself. The power of God is not an identical expression with the God of power; nor is the wisdom of God identical with the God of wisdom. The holy soul, in its contemplative state, loves to unite itself with God, considered as the subject of His attributes. It is not infinite wisdom, infinite power, or infinite goodness, considered separately from the existence of whom they can be predicated, which it loves and adores; but the God of infinite wisdom, power, and goodness.

ARTICLE TWENTY- EIGHTH

Christ is "the way, and the truth, and the life." The grace which sanctifies as well as that which justifies, is by Him and through Him. He is the true and living way; and no man can gain the victory over sin, and be brought into union with God, without Christ. And when, in some mitigated sense, we may be said to have arrived at the end of the way by being brought home to the Divine fold and reinstated in the Divine image, it would be sad indeed if we should forget the way itself, as Christ is sometimes called. At every period of our progress, however advanced it may be, our life is derived from God through Him and for Him. The most advanced souls are those which are most possessed with the thoughts and the presence of Christ.

Any other view would be extremely pernicious. It would be to snatch from the faithful eternal life, which consists in knowing the only true God and Jesus Christ His Son, whom he has sent.

ARTICLE TWENTY-NINTH

The way of holiness is wonderful, but it is not miraculous. Those in it, walk by simple faith alone. And perhaps there is nothing more remarkable nor wonderful in it, than that a result so great should be produced by a principle so simple.

When persons have arrived at the state of divine union, so that, in accordance with the prayer of the Saviour, they are made one with Christ in God, they no longer seem to put forth distinct inward acts, but their state appears to be characterized by a deep and Divine repose.

The continuous act is the act of faith, which brings into moral and religious union with the Divine nature; faith which, through the plenitude of Divine grace, is kept firm, unbroken.

The appearance of absolute continuity and unity in this blessed state is increased perhaps by the entire freedom of the mind from all eager, anxious, unquiet acts. The soul is not only at unity with itself in the respects which have been mentioned, but it has also a unity of rest.

This state of continuous faith and of consequent repose in God is sometimes denominated the passive state. The soul, at such times, ceases to originate acts which precede the grace of God. The decisions of her consecrated judgment, are the voice of the Holy Ghost in the soul. But if she first listens passively, it is subsequently her business to yield an active and effective cooperation in the line of duty which they indicate. The more pliant and supple the soul is to the Divine suggestions, the more real and efficacious is her own action, though without any excited and troubled movement. The more a soul receives from God, the more she ought to restore to Him of what she has from Him. This ebbing and flowing, if one may so express it, this communication on the part of God and the correspondent action on the part of man, constitute the order of grace on the one hand, and the action and fidelity of the creature on the other.

ARTICLE THIRTIETH

It would be a mistake to suppose, that the highest state of inward experience is characterized by great excitements, by raptures and ecstasies, or by any movements of feeling which would be regarded as particularly extraordinary.

One of the remarkable results in a soul of which faith is the sole governing principle, is, that it is entirely peaceful. Nothing disturbs it. And being thus peaceful, it reflects distinctly and clearly the image of Christ; like the placid lake, which shows, in its own clear and beautiful bosom, the exact forms of the objects around and above it. Another is, that having full faith in God and divested of all selfishness and resistance in itself, it is perfectly accessible and pliable to all the impressions of grace.

ARTICLE THIRTY-FIRST

It does not follow, that those who possess the graces of a truly sanctified heart, are at liberty to reject the ordinary methods and rules of perception and judgment. They exercise and value wisdom, while they reject the selfishness of wisdom. The rules of holy living would require them every moment to make a faithful use of all the natural light of reason, as well as the higher and spiritual light of grace.

A holy soul values and seeks wisdom, but does not seek it in an unholy and worldly spirit. Nor, when it is made wise by the Spirit of wisdom, who dwells in all hearts that are wholly devoted to God, does it turn back from the giver to the gift, and rejoice in its wisdom as its own.

The wisdom of the truly holy soul is a wisdom which estimates things in the present moment. It judges of duty from the facts which now are; including, however, those things which have a relation to the present. It is an important remark, that the present moment necessarily possesses a moral extension; so that, in judging of it, we are to include all those things which have a natural and near relation to the thing actually in hand. It is in this manner that the holy soul lives in the present, committing the past to God, and leaving the future with that approaching hour which shall convert it into the present. "Sufficient to the day is the evil thereof." To-morrow will take care of itself; it will bring, at its coming, its appropriate grace and light. When we live thus, God will not fail to give us our daily bread.

Such souls draw on themselves the special protection of Providence, under whose care they live, without a far extended and unquiet forecast, like little children resting in the bosom of their mother. Conscious of their own limited views, and keeping in mind the direction of the Saviour, Judge not that you be not judged, they are slow to pass judgment upon others. They are willing to receive reproof and correction; and, separate from the will of God, they have no choice or will of their own in anything.

These are the children whom Christ permits to come near Him. They combine the prudence of the serpent with the simplicity of the dove. But they do not appropriate their prudence to themselves as their own prudence, any more than they appropriate to themselves the beams of the natural sun, when they walk in its light.

These are the poor in spirit, whom Christ Jesus hath declared blessed; and who are as much taken off from any complacency in what others might call their merits, as all Christians ought to be from their temporal possessions. They are the "little ones," to whom God is well pleased to reveal His mysteries, while He hides them from the wise and prudent.

ARTICLE THIRTY-SECOND

The children, in distinction from the mere servants of God, have the liberty of children. They have a peace and joy, full of innocency. They take with simplicity and without hesitation the refreshments both of mind and body. They do not speak of themselves, except when called to do it in providence, and in order to do good. And such is their simplicity and truth of spirit, they speak of things just as they appear to them at the moment; and when the conversation turns upon their own works, or characters, they express themselves favorably or unfavorably, much as they would if they were speaking of others. If; however, they have occasion to speak of any good of which they have been the instrument, they always acknowledge, with humble joy, that it comes from God alone.

There is a liberty, which might more properly be called license. There are persons who maintain that purity of heart renders pure, in the subjects of this purity, whatever they are prompted to do, however irregular it may be in others. This is a great error.

ARTICLE THIRTY-THIRD

It is the doctrine of Augustine, as also of Thomas Aquinas, that the principle of holy love existing in the heart, necessarily includes in itself; or implies the existence, of all other Christian virtues. He who loves God with all his heart, will not violate the laws of purity, because it would be a disregard of the will of God, which he loves above all things. His love, under such circumstances, becomes the virtue of chastity. He has too much love and reverence for the will of God to murmur or repine under the dispensations of His providence. His love, under such circumstances, becomes the virtue of patience. And thus this love becomes by turns, on their appropriate occasions, all the virtues. As his love is perfect, so the virtues which flow out of it, and are modified from it, will not be less so.

It is a maxim in the doctrines of holiness, that the holy soul is crucified to its own virtues, although it possesses them in the highest degree. The meaning of this saying is this: The holy soul is so crucified to self in all its forms, that it practices the virtues without taking complacency in its virtues as it, own, and even without thinking how virtuous it is.

ARTICLE THIRTY-FORTH

The Apostle Paul speaks of Christians as dead. "You are dead," he says, "and your life is hid with Christ in God." (Col. iii. 3. These expressions will apply, in their full import, only to those Christians who are in the state of unselfish or pure love. Their death is a death to selfishness. They are dead to pride and jealousy, self-seeking and envy, to malice, inordinate love of their own reputation, anything and everything which constitutes the fallen and vitiated life of nature. They have a new life, which is "hid with Christ in God."

ARTICLE THIRTY-FIFTH

Some persons of great piety, in describing the highest religious state, have denominated it the state of transformation. But this can be regarded as only a synonymous expression for the state of pure love.

In the transformed state of the soul, as in the state of pure love, love is its life. In this principle of love all the affections of the soul, of whatever character, have their constituting or their controlling element. There can be no love without an object of love. As the principle of love, therefore, allies the soul with another, so from that other which is God, all its power of movement proceeds. In itself it remains without preference for anything; and consequently is accessible and pliant to all the touches and guidances of grace, however slight they may be. It is like a spherical body, placed upon a level and even surface, which is moved with equal ease in any direction. The soul in this state, having no preferences of itself, has but one principle of movement, namely, that which God gives it. In this state the soul can say with the Apostle Paul, "I live; Yet not I, but Christ lives in me."

ARTICLE THIRTY-SIXTH

Souls which have experienced the grace of sanctification in its higher degrees, have not so much need of set times arid places for worship as others. Such is the purity and the strength of their love, that it is very easy for them to unite with God in acts of inward worship, at all times and places. They have an interior closet. The soul is their temple, and God dwells in it.

This, however, does not exempt them from those outward methods and observances which God has prescribed. Besides, they owe something to others; and a disregard to the ordinances and ministrations of the Church could not fail to be injurious to beginners in the religions life.

ARTICLE THIRTY-SEVENTH

The practice of confession is not inconsistent with the state of pure love. The truly renovated soul can still say, Forgive us our trespasses. If it does not sin now, deliberately and knowingly, still its former state of sin can never be forgotten.

ARTICLE THIRTY-EIGHTH

In the transformed state, or state of pure love, there should be not only the confession of sins, properly so called, but also the confession of those more venial transgressions, termed faults. We should sincerely disapprove such faults in our confession; should condemn them and desire their remission; and not merely with a view to our own cleansing and deliverance, but also because God wills it, and because He would have us to do it for His glory.

ARTICLE THIRTY-NINTH

It is sometimes the case, that persons misjudge of the holiness of individuals, by estimating it from the incidents of the outward appearance. Holiness is consistent with the existence, in the same person, of various infirmities; (such as an unprepossessing form, physical weakness, a debilitated judgment, an imperfect mode of expression, defective manners, a want of knowledge, and the like.)

ARTICLE FORTIETH

The holy soul may be said to be united with God, without anything intervening or producing a separation, in three particulars.

First. It is thus united intellectually;-that is to say, not by any idea which is based upon the senses, and which of course could give only a material image of God, but by an idea which is internal and spiritual in its origin, and makes God known to us as a Being without form.

Second. The soul is thus united to God, if we may so express it, affectionately. That is to say, when its affections are given to God, not indirectly through a self-interested motive, but simply because He is what He is. The soul is united to God in love without anything intervening, when it loves Him for His own sake.

Third. The soul is thus united to God practically; and this is the case when it does the will of God, not by simply following a prescribed form, but from the constantly operative impulse of holy love.

ARTICLE FORTY-FIRST

We find in some devout writers on inward experience, the phrase spiritual nuptials. It is a favorite method with some of these writers, to represent the union of the soul with God by the figure of the bride and the bridegroom. Similar expressions are found in the Scriptures.

We are not to suppose that such expressions mean anything more, in reality, than that intimate union which exists between God and the soul, when the soul is in the state of pure love.

ARTICLE FORTY-SECOND

We find again other forms of expression, which it is proper to notice. The union between God and the soul is sometimes described by them as an "essential" union, and sometimes as a "substantial" union, as if there were a union of essence, substance, or being, in the literal or physical sense. They mean to express nothing more than the fact of the union of pure love, with the additional idea that the union is firm and established; not subject to those breaks and inequalities, to that want of continuity and uniformity of love which characterize inferior degrees of experience.

ARTICLE FORTY-THIRD

It is the holy soul of which St. Paul may be understood especially to speak, where he says, "As many as are led by the Spirit of God, they are the sons of God." (Rom. viii. 14.)

Those who are in a state of simple faith, which can always be said of those who are in the state of pure love, are the "little ones" of the Scriptures, of whom we are told that God teaches them. "I thank you, says the Saviour, "O Father, Lord of heaven and earth, that you have hid these things from the wise and prudent, and has revealed them to babes." (Luke x. 21.) Such souls, taught as they are by the Spirit of God which dwells in them, possess a knowledge which the wisdom of the world could never impart. But such knowledge never renders them otherwise than respectful to religious teachers, docile to the instructions of the Church, and conformable in all things to the precepts of the Scriptures.

ARTICLE FORTY-FOURTH

The doctrine of pure love has been known and recognized as a true doctrine among the truly contemplative and devout in all ages of the Church. The doctrine, however, has been so far above the common experience, that the pastors and saints of all ages have exercised a degree of discretion and care in making it known, except to those to whom God had already given both the attraction and light to receive it. Acting on the principle of giving milk to infants and strong meat to those that were more advanced, they addressed in the great body of Christians the motives of fear and of hope, founded on the consideration of happiness or of misery. It seemed to them, that the motive of God's glory, in itself considered, a motive which requires us to love God for Himself alone without a distinct regard and reference to our own happiness, could he profitably addressed, as a general rule, only to those who are somewhat advanced in inward experience.

ARTICLE FORTY-FIFTH

Among the various forms of expression indicative of the highest experience, we sometimes find that of "Divine union," or "union with God."

Union with God, not a physical but moral or religious union, necessarily exists in souls that are in the state of pure love. The state of "Divine union "is not a higher state than that of pure love, but may rather be described as the same state.

Strive after it; but do not too readily or easily believe that you have attained to it. The traveler, after many fatigues and dangers, arrives at the top of a mountain. As he looks abroad from that high eminence, and in that clear atmosphere, he sees his native city; and it seems to him to be very near. Overjoyed at the sight, and perhaps deceived by his position, he proclaims himself as already at the end of his journey. But he soon finds that the distance was greater than he supposed. He is obliged to descend into valleys, and to climb over hills, and to surmount rugged rocks, and to wind his tired steps over many a mile of weary way, before he reaches that home and city, which he once thought so near.

It is thus in relation to the sanctification of the heart. True holiness of heart is the object at which the Christian aims. He beholds it before him, as an object of transcendent beauty, and as perhaps near at hand. But as he advances towards it, he finds the way longer and more difficult than he had imagined. But if on the one hand we should be careful not to mistake au intermediate stopping place for the end of the way, we should be equally careful on the other not to be discouraged by the difficulties we meet with; remembering that the obligation to be holy is always binding upon us, and that God will help those who put their trust in Him.

"Whatsoever is born of God, overcomes the world; and this is the victory that overcomes the world, EVEN OUR FAITH." (1 John v.4.)

Printed in Great Britain
by Amazon